Wild Animal Babies

pictures by Carl and Mary Hauge

A GOLDEN BOOK · NEW YORK
Western Publishing Company, Inc.
Racine, Wisconsin 53404

The babies play while Father LION
and Mother LION watch over them.

When baby **ELEPHANTS** are in the water, they like to spray each other.

Very tall grass is a favorite play-ground for baby RHINOCEROSES.

Baby BEARS—and big BEARS, too—

love to eat honey and blueberries.

ZEBRAS look like black-and-white-striped horses. So do their babies.

When they grow up, these baby
GIRAFFES will eat leaves from the
very tallest trees.

Baby HIPPOPOTAMUS lives where it is very hot. She and her mother keep cool by standing in water.

Baby OPOSSUMS ride everywhere
on their mother's back.

Baby DEER takes a drink from the stream.

Baby RACCOONS are curious.
They like to feel things.

The hot, dry desert is where
Baby CAMEL lives.

Baby BISON lives on the rolling prairie.

From Mother's pouch, Baby
KANGAROO watches Sister
play with her friend.

Baby FOXES learn to hunt by chasing grasshoppers and crickets.

Treetops are the home of these baby MONKEYS.

Mother POLAR BEAR teaches her
baby how to swim.

Baby BEAVER helps her family
to build a new home.

Baby SEALS love to play together in the water.

The TIGER cubs are out for a walk
with their mother.

After playing and eating, baby animals
like to sleep. Good night, babies.